Little People, BIG DREAMS
EVONNE GOOLAGONG

Written by
Maria Isabel Sánchez Vegara

Illustrated by
Lisa Koesterke

Frances Lincoln
Children's Books

Little Evonne grew up on a hot, dusty farm in Australia. She was the third of eight children, all of them descendants of the Wiradjuri people, who had lived on the land for more than 60,000 years.

Evonne's family was very poor and couldn't afford to buy her many toys. But one day, under the wheel of her father's car, Evonne found the most amazing treasure: an old tennis ball.

She loved that tennis ball so much! Her father made her a wooden racket to hit it with. It didn't look like the real thing, "But I can start with anything!" Evonne thought.

One evening, she discovered a story about a young female tennis player who went to a place in England called Wimbledon and won on its magical center court. She went to bed dreaming about that girl.

But taking part in a world-class tennis tournament felt like a fairy tale to a little Indigenous girl! Evonne was not allowed to join a tennis club and had to watch the games through the fence, memorizing everything the coach said.

Evonne went to the club day after day. Finally, the club's manager noticed her. He gave her the keys so that she could teach herself how to play when all the kids were gone. And she did!

A tennis coach named Vic Edwards heard about a young girl who could play faster than any other new talent. He asked Evonne to move to Sydney. There, she lived with his family and trained to become a professional player.

The day she left home, her mother gave Evonne a tennis dress made of bedsheets and some very good advice: "Do not worry about winning or losing. Just play your best and have a lovely time."

It became Evonne's secret weapon! She didn't think winning was everything and losing was a disaster. Every time she hit the court, she enjoyed her matches and looked forward to the next point.

AUSTRALIAN OPEN

US OPEN ● US OPEN

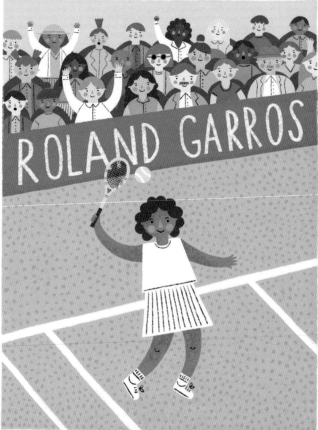

ROLAND GARROS

Shot after shot, Evonne made it into all the major tournaments, playing in Sydney, Paris, and New York. One day...she was in Wimbledon! She won the tournament and became number one in the world.

She had to wait nine years until she won Wimbledon again. That day, there was a very special guest watching her from the stands—her daughter Kelly. Evonne became the first mother to win the tournament in more than 60 years.

When she retired, Evonne kept inspiring the next generation of Australian tennis players, helping young Indigenous children make it onto the court.

HAMPIONSHIP

And this is how little Evonne became the most graceful player the world has ever met. A living legend who breaks barriers every time she hits the ball.

EVONNE GOOLAGONG

(Born 1951)

1960

1971

Evonne Fay Goolagong was born on July 31, 1951, to Wiradjuri people in Barellan, a small town in New South Wales, Australia. Evonne is an Indigenous Australian, meaning that she is a descendant of Australia's first people who have lived on the land for more than 60,000 years. When Evonne was a little girl, Indigenous Australians were treated very poorly by white people, who did not recognize their heritage. They were also not allowed to enjoy many everyday things that white people did—like playing tennis. Luckily, the owner of the local club ignored this rule, and it was a good thing he did. Evonne was faster than any other child her age, and she had an amazing ability to judge a tennis ball's speed and bounce. Evonne's biggest

1980   2018

dream was to play on Wimbledon's center court. In 1956, her dream
became reality when she was spotted by professional tennis coach
Vic Edwards. He had heard about Evonne's skill and suggested she
move to Sydney to train and become professional. Within months,
she was Junior Australian Champion, and at age 20, she beat fellow
Australian Margaret Court in Wimbledon, becoming the number one
player in the world. Evonne went on to win 92 tournaments, including
Wimbledon and the Australian Open. Understanding that "your
dreams when you are little are the force that keeps you going," Evonne
now helps hundreds of young Indigenous athletes find their way on—
and off—the tennis court.

Want to find out more about **Evonne Goolagong?**
Read one of these great books:

Home!: The Evonne Goolagong Story by Evonne Goolagong Cawley and Phil Jarratt

Evonne!: On the Move by Evonne Goolagong with Bud Collins

BOARD BOOKS

COCO	MAYA	FRIDA	AMELIA	MARIE	ADA	ROSA	EMMELINE	AUDREY	ELLA

978-1-78603-245-4 978-1-78603-249-2 978-1-78603-247-8 978-1-78603-252-2 978-1-78603-253-9 978-1-78603-259-1 978-1-78603-263-8 978-1-78603-261-4 978-1-78603-255-3 978-1-78603-257-7

BOOKS & PAPER DOLLS

EMMELINE PANKHURST
ISBN: 978-1-78603-400-7

MARIE CURIE
ISBN: 978-1-78603-401-4

BOX SETS

WOMEN IN ART

WOMEN IN SCIENCE

ISBN: 978-1-78603-428-1   ISBN: 978-1-78603-429-8

Collect the
Little People, **BIG DREAMS** series:

FRIDA KAHLO	COCO CHANEL	MAYA ANGELOU	AMELIA EARHART	AGATHA CHRISTIE	MARIE CURIE

ISBN: 978-1-84780-783-0   ISBN: 978-1-84780-784-7   ISBN: 978-1-84780-889-9   ISBN: 978-1-84780-888-2   ISBN: 978-1-84780-960-5   ISBN: 978-1-84780-962-9

ROSA PARKS

ISBN: 978-1-78603-018-4

AUDREY HEPBURN

ISBN: 978-1-78603-053-5

EMMELINE PANKHURST

ISBN: 978-1-78603-020-7

ELLA FITZGERALD

ISBN: 978-1-78603-087-0

ADA LOVELACE

ISBN: 978-1-78603-076-4

JANE AUSTEN
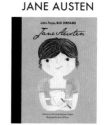
ISBN: 978-1-78603-120-4

GEORGIA O'KEEFFE

ISBN: 978-1-78603-122-8

HARRIET TUBMAN

ISBN: 978-1-78603-227-0

ANNE FRANK

ISBN: 978-1-78603-229-4

MOTHER TERESA

ISBN: 978-1-78603-230-0

JOSEPHINE BAKER

ISBN: 978-1-78603-228-7

L. M. MONTGOMERY
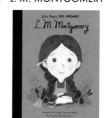
ISBN: 978-1-78603-233-1

JANE GOODALL

ISBN: 978-1-78603-231-7

SIMONE DE BEAUVOIR

ISBN: 978-1-78603-232-4

MUHAMMAD ALI

ISBN: 978-1-78603-331-4

STEPHEN HAWKING

ISBN: 978-1-78603-333-8

MARIA MONTESSORI

ISBN: 978-1-78603-755-8

VIVIENNE WESTWOOD

ISBN: 978-1-78603-757-2

MAHATMA GANDHI

ISBN: 978-1-78603-787-9

DAVID BOWIE

ISBN: 978-1-78603-332-1

WILMA RUDOLPH
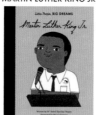
ISBN: 978-1-78603-751-0

DOLLY PARTON

ISBN: 978-1-78603-760-2

BRUCE LEE

ISBN: 978-0-7112-4629-4

RUDOLF NUREYEV

ISBN: 978-1-78603-791-6

ZAHA HADID
ISBN: 978-0-7112-4641-6

MARY SHELLEY
ISBN: 978-0-7112-4639-3

MARTIN LUTHER KING JR.
ISBN: 978-0-7112-4567-9

DAVID ATTENBOROUGH
ISBN: 978-0-7112-4564-8

ASTRID LINDGREN
ISBN: 978-0-7112-5217-2

EVONNE GOOLAGONG
ISBN: 978-0-7112-4586-0

Brimming with creative inspiration, how-to projects, and useful information to enrich your everyday life, Quarto Knows is a favorite destination for those pursuing their interests and passions. Visit our site and dig deeper with our books into your area of interest: Quarto Creates, Quarto Cooks, Quarto Homes, Quarto Lives, Quarto Drives, Quarto Explores, Quarto Gifts, or Quarto Kids.

Text © 2020 Maria Isabel Sánchez Vegara. Illustrations © 2020 Lisa Koesterke.

First Published in the USA in 2020 by Frances Lincoln Children's Books, an imprint of The Quarto Group.

400 First Avenue North, Suite 400, Minneapolis, MN 55401, USA.

T (612) 344-8100 F (612) 344-8692 **www.QuartoKnows.com**

First Published in Spain in 2019 under the title Pequeña & Grande Evonne Goolagong

by Alba Editorial, s.l.u., Baixada de Sant Miquel, 1, 08002 Barcelona

www.albaeditorial.es

All rights reserved.

Published by arrangement with Alba Editorial, s.l.u. Translation rights arranged by IMC Agència Literària, SL

All rights reserved.

A catalog record for this book is available from the British Library.

ISBN 978-0-7112-4586-0

Set in Futura BT.

Published by Katie Cotton • Designed by Karissa Santos

Edited by Rachel Williams and Katy Flint • Production by Caragh McAleenan

Manufactured in Guangdong, China CC122019

9 7 5 3 1 2 4 6 8

Photographic acknowledgments (pages 28–29, from left to right) 1.Tennis pro Evonne Goolagong with racket, 1960 © Keystone Press / Alamy Stock Photo 2. International tennis championships in Hilversum, Evonne Goolagong (winner) with cup, 1971 © Photo collection Anefo / National Archives, CC0 3. Evonne Goolagong Cawley v Tracy Austin - 1980 Wimbledon Championships, 1980 © Photo by Eamonn McCabe/Popperfoto via Getty Images. 4. Australia Day Honours List recipient Evonne Goolagong Cawley poses for a photo with her Companion in the General Division of the Order of Australia (AC) award on day 13 of the 2018 Australian Open at Melbourne Park on January 27, 2018, in Melbourne, Australia © Quinn Rooney/Getty Images)

MIX
Paper from responsible sources
FSC® C008047